Tap into Ancestral Healing

Clearing your past, transforming your present and creating your magical future with EFT

Jacqui Crooks

First published in Great Britain 2022 by Purple Star Publishing

Design by Clare McCabe, www.purplestardesign.co.uk

ISBN13: 978-1-3999-1893-0

DISCLAIMER

The contents of this book do not constitute advice and is not intended as a substitute for professional medical or business advice.
This book is published in good faith but neither the publisher or the author shall be held liable for any alleged damage arising from any suggestion or information contained in this book.

Dedication

I'd like to dedicate this book to my family, past, present and future. They are why I'm this version of me and why I created the work that turned into this book. My grateful thanks for each and everyone of you, right back through time and forward to those who aren't yet born. May our journeys be joyous :)

Contents

Forward

The present moment is all we have - now is the only time we have in which to take action. But acknowledging the roots of our challenges from the past provides a powerful opportunity for healing in the present, and a much greater level of freedom in the future.

Of the many EFT practitioners I've had the pleasure to know, I don't know of anyone more gifted in addressing these pre-packaged issues than Jacqui Crooks.

I had the privilege and pleasure of coaching Jacqui in the relatively early days of my career. I had only recently been building my presence online, allowing me to reach an international audience, and was still a year or two away from shooting my first YouTube video. I was instantly charmed by her, and saw the warmth and compassion that would be of great benefit to so many people. It was exciting to learn, just a year or so later, that Jacqui had qualified to become one of the Founding EFT Masters.

It is also a privilege and a pleasure to be able to introduce this book you are now going to experience. Jacqui has taken her years of experience and created a lovely guide to support you in clearing those past experiences that may have been limiting your health, wealth and happiness. I found both the examples of clients and the tapping suggestions very useful, and I know I will be using some of Jacqui's insights in my future work. Whether you are tapping for yourself, or you are a practitioner helping others, I trust you will likewise find this book very helpful.

I'm confident that you, like me, will be grateful to Jacqui for sharing her wisdom in this book. Congratulations on picking it up - now enjoy!

Be Magnificent!

Brad Yates

www.tapwithbrad.com

"If you've not yet met Brad, I'd like to introduce you to an amazing tapper and all round great guy :) if you like tapping, please follow him, he has more tapping videos than anyone I know and they really hit the spot :)" **Jacqui Crooks**

Introduction

This book has been created to show you how to free yourself from anything you're carrying that's not yours. All the old family beliefs, strategies, world views that were created by other people, living other lives, at other times, that you've inherited, along with the colour of your hair and the shape of your nose. Unlike your hair and nose, you can, thankfully, do something about the inherited beliefs and life is much easier and happier when you do.

Most of the things we find a problem in our life right now, were created by someone else as a solution to a problem they had and it doesn't work for us any longer, because we're different people, with different skills and understanding and the world is a very different place. I'll explain more about this in Chapter 2 before we tap to clear the things that aren't ours, in Chapter 3.

The book is written for both those of you who are EFT practitioners, to enhance your skills, while clearing old "stuff" and for those of you who want to use these skills for yourself. There is a quick guide to using EFT at the back of the book and a YouTube video too, if you're not already familiar with EFT.

I will show you how to create a magical rebirth in Chapter 4, so your subconscious has new, helpful resources to refer to. We'll look at and clear possible past life traumas in Chapter 5. Don't worry if you don't have past life memories, we can clear the trauma anyway. We'll look at and clear the trauma and unhelpful beliefs about yourself and the world, that you've created in your life, the things that are getting in your way right now in Chapter 6, 7.

Finally, in Chapter 8, I share with you how to design your future, really feeling into the life you want to live and we create a template, to help your subconscious guide you to it. This book is a one stop shop, to letting go what's not yours, so you can create the life you want, so you can be your real self, feeling safe to shine your light in the world, letting your golden soul shine out. We need you, so please join me and let your light shine out :)

www.jacquicrooks.com
https://www.youtube.com/user/jaquicrooks

Life's journey

If you've found this book, then I'm guessing you're also on the journey of getting to know who you are and your place in the world and I'm looking forward to sharing part of this journey with you.

My journey, like yours, has been life long, although it was many years before I saw it that way. I've learnt, and rebelled and learnt some more. I've learnt, in spite of me and because of me and I'm finally allowing myself to see the journey as a growing into me and to give myself credit for my efforts and my persistence, rather than my old pattern of beating myself up because "I should have known better," "I should have done things differently," "I should have done it sooner," and all the "if onlys." I'm sure you recognise those patterns :)

As I say to my clients, and I'm finally acknowledging it applies to me as well:-

> *"We are always in the right place, at the right time, doing the right thing, with the*

right people."

As my friend David Hamilton says, "We can only do it right."

So here we are, in the right place, at the right time, doing the right thing, with the right people.

Let's have fun as we share this time together!

Those of you who know me, or have worked with me, will know that I like to help people to clear the "stuff" they're carrying that isn't theirs.

I use the word "stuff" frequently, by the way, because it covers a multitude of things and it allows the subconscious to decide which of those things are relevant, without us having to consciously know what they are.

I've been using EFT since 1999 and the way I use it has changed enormously in that time, thanks to the things that I've learned from working with my clients. I was, I think, in the first group in the UK to learn EFT and you can imagine what it was like, when no one had ever heard of it, asking people to tap on themselves, and at that time, to hum and count as well! It was a little challenging!

I was a primary school teacher for many years, specialising in working with four year olds, although in my time I worked with every age from three to eleven.

I decided it was time to move onto something new, though I wasn't sure what and then I came across hypnotherapy, definitely a case of being in the right place, at the right time, with the right people.

That first weekend of hypnotherapy training was like coming home. It just felt so right. I made two very good friends on the course and we practised with each other every week. Perfect for clearing "stuff" as you learn.

I became a practitioner, put my advert into Yellow Pages, the business phone book, this was before the internet, sat back and waited for clients to find me! I really did think it was as simple as that!

Eventually clients did find me and I loved working with them, it felt like this was what I was here to do .... And then, in a supervision session, my trainer, Peter Delves, asked if he could try out a strange new technique that he'd learnt. Of course, I said yes, and the rest is history. It was EFT and the shifts I had in that practice session blew me away. I asked when he'd be training in EFT so he set up his first training and I was on it. After that I helped him with his trainings, until he suggested I train as a trainer, so I did. By this time, I had quite a busy hypnotherapy practice and I was trying to persuade people to tap instead! In the end, I pre-framed, "We may use this new technique that allows you to do everything you do in hypnosis, without spending time going into trance, and the best thing is, I can teach you to use it yourself."

It worked. People came for EFT and I found that all the things I'd learnt in my Hypnosis and NLP training were seamlessly transferring themselves to EFT, without me consciously having to do that.

EFT is so different now from the early days! We started, not knowing what the outcome would be, feeling our way through situations with clients, believing EFT would make a difference, and not being sure quite how, or what was happening when change came. We didn't always know what we'd done to make a change with one client, when it didn't work with another. We created all sorts of theories.

As the years have gone on and we've worked with more and more clients on more and more issues, we've each created a way of using EFT that works for us and our clients. We probably have a million different ways of viewing why EFT works, depending on our background and our previous skills.

As my background was in hypnotherapy and NLP and before that an Infant teacher specialising in teaching four year olds - which was very helpful when working with resistant parts - my view of the way that I use EFT is that I use it to allow me to connect directly to the subconscious, to give it new information.

The subconscious is always happy to do its best for you, if it knows what that is. Often it doesn't; it's running on old, outdated information, maybe picked up in the womb from family, or picked up in early childhood.

Imagine if you were trying to use your computer to host webinars or talk to people on zoom and it still had the software and memory that it had in 1998. You wouldn't expect it to be able to do a good job for you, would you? You'd want to add new memory, update the software and that way it will be able to do what you want it to do, easily and quickly and you'll be happy about that.

How I view EFT is as a way to update the software, to give new information, more memory, new programs and to delete the outdated programs that are no longer needed.

I do that by tapping, while using my hypnotherapy and NLP skills to talk to the subconscious.

Others will use EFT in different ways, depending on their particular skills and that's ok. There are as many ways to use EFT as there are people using it. And it's all OK. The important thing is, does it work? For you? And if you're a practitioner, for your clients? And if it does, you're doing a great job, and if it doesn't? You're still doing a great job and how could you use it differently to get the results that you want?

When I first started using EFT I had to tap on my guilt because I realised that clients who would come to me a few years later, would have a better experience with me than my current clients. I tapped to reframe it by reminding myself that if I didn't practice on these people no one would ever get a better experience.

And then I asked the universe for challenges, so I could learn more and learn more quickly. If you do that, be warned the universe will take you at your word!!

I had so many different clients with so many different issues. There were rebels, who were silently going "you can't make me," and of course they were right. Luckily, having a very strong rebel myself, I did have empathy with them and working with them helped me to create new ways of working, that got the rebel on board. A reformed rebel can be a very useful thing and the rebel qualities can be used in many helpful ways.

There were the helpless and hopeless, the ones who came with the story that "nothing" works for me and of course with that belief, they were right, nothing did.

I became very skilled at working with Parts and with the Inner Children who were running the show from their childhood perspectives and it was fascinating and sometimes frustrating, and I was learning, learning, learning all the time.

I rarely had clients presenting with simple issues and I was glad, because it seemed to me that all issues had deeper roots than showed on the surface, and the deeper the clearing, the greater the change and the more permanent it was.

Even apparently simple phobias often turned out to have complex roots and to clear them completely required detective work. That's what I realised I was, a detective, and I still see my journey with a client as two detectives looking for clues and putting them together to make sense of what doesn't make sense, so we can make changes.

A good illustration of how important detective work is, are flight phobias. I have worked on a flight phobia that was simple: it started after a flight with bad turbulence. We dealt with the trauma and what they made it mean, and the phobia cleared. I had a flight phobia that started when the person had had a baby and was terrified if something went wrong, they couldn't save the baby. Someone else also started the phobia when he had a baby, but this was because he was travelling for work and if he died, he wouldn't be there for the baby, and that linked back to his dad not being there for him as a child and his fear of not being a good dad.

There was someone who had a fear of there being nothing firm beneath his feet when he was flying, which linked to not having support when he was young.

There was someone who had her first flight just after she'd lost her husband and was still in a state of grief and fear, and somehow her subconscious had thought flying and the grief and fear were linked, so every time she flew, those feelings came back.

We discovered those aspects by tapping on the feelings and the subconscious kindly brought up thoughts and images and yet more feelings for us to work with. Once we tracked the issues back to the roots, it was easy to use EFT to clear them and it's the good detective work that you can do with EFT that will help you to uncover the underlying roots.

It was this detective work that first got me to dealing with very early traumas. I used client's feelings to get back as early as we could, to clear traumas and beliefs where they started and then I found that sometimes even going back to early childhood wasn't far enough back, so I started working with the things that were picked up in the womb, and then I recognised that many of the things we were carrying weren't ours in the first place; they had come down the family line and we took them on as ours, before we had the understanding that they weren't. I also started to explore the place of past lives, in the things we're dealing with now.

This was where my hypnotherapy and NLP training came in so useful. Using what Milton Erickson called "artfully vague" language, I found it was possible to offer the client's subconscious suggestions of things that might have happened and tap to give it permission to clear that, or anything that had been picked up that was no longer for the clients' highest good. I found ways to clear early issues even when it wasn't possible to know exactly what they were, which really made a huge difference to the results we could achieve.

I practised using language in ways that gave instructions to the subconscious, gave different parts of the client new information and sometimes new jobs, and I could really see how things cleared at a much deeper level and much more quickly than they had before.

In this book, as well as reminding you who you really are, I am sharing with you the ways I use EFT to make a difference, and I invite you to play with some of the concepts here to see how they work for you.

The way I've laid this out will take you through the process of clearing what's not yours and what's no longer helpful to you, give new, useful information to your subconscious, so it can do a great job for you and help you to get clear about what you want and how to attract it.

Take whatever you like and customise it so it works for you. EFT is a great deliverer of skills that you already have and you have many more skills than you realise.

So, have a play with the concepts in the book, make it light hearted, invite your Parts to play with you, to come up with creative ways to use the ideas.

Above all, have fun. Try it with yourself, try it with friends, try it with clients. Notice what you're not comfortable with and tap on that. You might like to check in with how it makes you feel. Where are you feeling that, what's that feeling like?

And then, if you choose, you can use the exercise in Chapter one to take yourself back to an early time that you had the same feeling and clear its roots.

Remember that you can do that, even if you don't consciously know where those feelings began.

When you're congruent with the way that you're using EFT, your clients, if you're a practitioner, will be comfortable using EFT in that way. If you find resistance from your clients, check what's going on for you, because there may be a part of you that's resistant. If you're working on yourself, also notice when you feel resistance and take time to explore why that might be.

Cherry pick from the book. What lights your fire? What feels exciting to you to explore? Go ahead and explore it, in your way, knowing that you can make adjustments whenever you need to.

And if you don't use anything in the book? Don't worry, it's all stored in the subconscious, and when you're relaxed and focusing on you or your client, anything from the book which would be useful for you will just pop out of your mouth, without your conscious mind getting in the way. As one of my American trainees found, it might even come out of your mouth with a British accent. Not a problem if you're British of course, but startling if you're not! So .... on we go ..... Let the fun commence :)

CHAPTER 1

Tapping

For suggestions of ways of using EFT see the Techniques appendix at the end of the book. You might choose to read the book first and then tap, or tap as you go along, or neither and you can be sure that what you're reading is being stored in your subconscious for whenever it's needed.

The essence of this book is to give you and your subconscious new information and to show you how to use EFT, or tapping, to do that. I will give many examples of ways that you can word things to clear out old unhelpful beliefs, feelings and stored traumas.

These statements are not a script to be followed come what may. They are an example of things that you can say. They might hit the spot for you and certainly tapping with these statements can help, and it's also likely that there are other things personal to you, that will fit you even better and can be added in, or used instead. Don't be afraid to use your own words, you are likely to be more on target if you do. And the worst that can happen is nothing happens. You can't get it wrong, it's always trial and error, in all that we do. "If I tap on this, does it feel better?" is the way to go.

Using my words is a great start and might be all you need, and using yours, adds to the experience.

Likewise, at the end of the statements, you can vary the wording. I like to add in somewhere, I deeply and completely accept myself, because if we really did, what we're working on wouldn't be a problem! And I mix it with "I'm OK," and "I love, forgive and accept myself." Try different wordings yourself; however, I would recommend somewhere having I deeply and completely accept myself.

It can be very easy to create words that are comfortable, because they're not really doing the job they were designed for, so they allow you to stay where you are, while thinking that you're changing things I deeply and completely accept myself, makes sure you stay on target.

For a simple way to use EFT, go to my YouTube channel, and there will be other ways discussed at the end of the book, in the appendix.

It may be useful to have a journal with you as you

read this book. You can brainstorm, ask yourself questions and answer yourself and note down new information that comes to light, ready for tapping. And there are other ways to do this if journalling isn't your thing.

If you do decide to use a journal, I'd like to suggest you might choose a beautiful one, something that lights you up, that you can't wait to write in. It makes the whole process so much more fun.

I find that sitting writing in a journal about what's happening in my life, how I'm feeling about it, really helpful. I start writing, really, just rambling and then as I write, thoughts pop up, inspiration appears, new thoughts, new connections, new ideas. Often the solution to a problem appears as if by magic, in a way that my logical, conscious mind could never have done.

Writing in this way, is really a way to connect to your subconscious and allow it to share the information it has, that your conscious mind knows nothing about. When you're working through a programme like this, it can also be helpful to keep track of what's happening, the thoughts, feelings, ideas that pop up for you, so you can check in that things have been completely cleared.

If a story I tell resonates, you could note it, for looking at later. If a feeling pops up as you're reading, you could note what you were reading that might have brought it up. It's all part of being a great detective. You never know where the clues will appear, and it's good to keep track of them. It allows you to work on one aspect, without losing track of other aspects that need work and of course, it's really satisfying to read back at the end of the process and see just how far you've come:)

And for those of you that journaling doesn't appeal to, you can just talk to yourself, or think your thoughts and your subconscious will do what needs to be done. You can even record yourself.

CHAPTER 2

Transforming Our Past

You are so much more than you think you are.

And some of what you think you are, is not you!

Did you know that who you are at this moment is the sum total of all that your parents and family and ancestors have experienced, right back to the dawn of time?

Did you know that experiences that you've had in other lives can still be influencing you in this life?

Did you realise that your beliefs and fears and ways of seeing the world are all about safety and survival?

Milton Erickson, the famous Hypnotherapist, from whom NLP was modelled, said that ***"All problems were once solutions"*** and the problems that we are dealing with in our lives now were once solutions to an ancestor of ours. Sometimes we'll know where these things come from - we see ourselves doing the same as our mum or our dad, but ...

Why did they do that?

Who did they model?

How far back down the line was that created?

We're unlikely to know, but that doesn't mean that we can't make changes here and now.

I used to believe that we learnt to be angry, or anxious, that we modelled the people around us and then I realised we could pick up anxiety from our mother in the womb.

I remember working with a client very early on in my career, who said that her mother had told her that she was born anxious. With the knowledge I had then, I suggested that she had learnt to be anxious from her anxious mother and grandmother. It didn't occur to me that she could have picked up the habit of anxiety in the womb and of course, that was exactly what she had done. She'd spent her time in the womb being flooded with her mother's adrenaline, and just like a drug addict's child, she was born addicted to the adrenaline. The difference was, her body knew how to make her drug of choice, adrenaline and so it did, hence the anxious baby.

I began to wonder what else we picked up in the womb, wondering is a very useful strategy, and realised that the mother and baby are so close, sharing so many things physically, that of course we must pick up all sorts of things during the time in the womb. We're feeling whatever our mother feels and that's influenced by what's going on around her and her feelings about that, and of course, the meaning that she makes about herself based on that.

What goes on for the mother will also depend on what goes on for the father and how he expresses that, and that's influenced by what their parents felt and expressed too.

Babies pick up an enormous amount in the womb, not just on the physical level.

The reason I started working in this way originally, was because of 2 clients that I was working with. They came to me separately, 2 weeks apart and both with what looked to be similar issues. They had a huge fear of rejection, which was running, and ruining, their lives. The fear was so great that they wouldn't risk going into a relationship, as the fear of the pain of rejection was so huge.

I worked with both of them, on early traumas, later traumas, anything and everything we could find that might be related to rejection, and no matter what we cleared, and we did clear huge traumatic stuff, the same feelings were there when they considered having a relationship and the possibility of rejection.

In the end, having asked the universe for inspiration, I asked one of the clients, more in desperation than anything else, "Are there any stories about your birth?"

"Oh yes, he said, my mother tried to abort me, but we have a very good relationship now."

The missing piece! Can you imagine what that foetus must have felt? In the womb of a desperate mother. Feeling her anxiety, maybe terror. The guilt and fear and sadness she must have been feeling, that, as a foetus, he must have been feeling too.

And more importantly than the trauma, are the beliefs that he created from it. The beliefs that he made about himself, his place in the world, about others and his connection with them.

Maybe a belief that he's not supposed to be here, that there's not a place for him in the world, that he causes distress to others just by being him, by being here, that he can't trust that anyone will love him.

And the decisions he may have made based on that. **"I'm never going to feel this again."" It's not safe to risk loving," "It's too painful."**

We tapped on the trauma of that time and the meanings that he made about it, **"I'm not wanted," "I'm not supposed to be here," "I'm not safe,"** and things changed. Just knowing there was a reason for the feelings helped, he didn't feel so powerless and gradually the fear changed and the thought of being in a relationship felt more possible.

Sometimes the change can be instantaneous and sometimes it's necessary to work to clear the habit of seeing the world and yourself in the old way before the change is apparent and you can tap directly on the habit. **"Even though I have this habit, I'm reminding all parts of me that we don't do this any more and I thank them for their help in letting this go now."**

Once we cleared the trauma and the beliefs, the sense of relief was huge, he even looked different.

So, when the second client came in, I decided to ask him the same question.

"Are there any stories about your birth?"

"Yes, my mum tried to abort me. I was a twin and my twin died and I survived."

Unbelievable! And yet it was what happened.

Can you imagine, not only was he dealing with the trauma of the attempted abortion, but with the grief of losing his twin and survivor guilt. It was as though the Universe was giving me a message, letting me know where to start looking for the deep roots of current issues. Again, as we cleared the trauma and the beliefs that came from this, the relief was huge. The client held himself differently, he even sounded different.

Although each client now had a loving connection with their mother, this initial trauma was still shaping how they saw themselves and their place in the world.

I have worked with many clients where their mother was shocked or scared or overwhelmed when they found that they were pregnant, and the child in the womb picked up on those feelings and created a belief that they weren't supposed to be here, or they didn't deserve to be here and they had lived their life as though that was true. They had tried to stay small, to be inconspicuous, to take up as little space in the world as possible and the thought of stepping into themselves, being visible, was terrifying. They literally thought that if anyone realised they were here, they'd die. You can see how limiting those beliefs were and how impossible it would be to be successful in business, or even in life if you are carrying them.

Some people who start life with that shock and create the belief that they aren't supposed to be here, spend their life partly or wholly out of their body. They can find it difficult to be clear about their feelings, because they aren't in their body to feel them. They don't have any grounding and can drift through life. Even if they make plans, they have no means of carrying them out. We're in this life to balance our spiritual nature with living in a physical world and if we're not in the world, it's difficult to do that successfully.

Experiments show that children have Delta brainwaves until they are around four, that's similar to being in deep hypnosis. It means the vast amounts of information that they are bombarded with can be loaded straight into the subconscious, where it's hardwired in. It's designed to give them the information they need to be safe in a strange new environment. Unfortunately, the subconscious doesn't reason. It doesn't consider whether the information is useful, out of date or dangerous; once it receives it, it uses it until it's told to stop!

Essentially all our problems link back to safety and survival, although they may show in many different guises. It was, after all, only as recently as the 1930s that people were facing starvation in the Depression and depending on your age, our parents, grandparents or great grandparents will be carrying memories of that.

Depending upon the area that you come from there will also be a whole lot of coping strategies for survival that people are carrying. If you come from Eastern Europe where there has been endless war, people attacking and being attacked, invading and being invaded, borders changing frequently, there will be people expressing victimhood and people expressing aggression. There may be a fear of being invaded, of losing what's yours. Maybe a need to cling to your tribe, your family. It's about safely and survival.

If you come from a Jewish background, when Jews have been persecuted not for hundreds of years, but for thousands, there may be suspicion, fear, a sense of being on the alert for the next attack, a waiting for someone to take everything from you, not being able to keep your loved ones safe.

For someone whose family has a background of slavery, there may be a sense of powerlessness, a fear of losing everything, a belief that you don't have what you need to stay safe.

Someone whose family comes from the UK, where our last major invasion was in 1066, will have different strategies to someone from mainland Europe, where an invasion can happen, just by driving a bit further along a road. In the UK we have a need to "Keep our head below the parapet", from the 1st world war, and "Know our place," Don't get too big for your boots," "Don't blow your own trumpet," all things said to a British child in childhood. To keep us small and invisible, so we don't get into trouble. Probably based on the feudal system, where to stand out made you visible and therefore a target, or a scapegoat. Try running a business with those instructions!!

And of course for all of these things, there will be parts of us rebelling and trying to create something different, while other parts will believe that something different isn't possible.

All those strategies were created many years ago, for good reasons and we're often still using them, without consciously recognising that or considering if they still serve us.

The good news is that that's all they are, coping strategies and when you can see what you do in your life as just that, rather than an essential part of you, it becomes much easier to change those strategies to something that supports you.

CHAPTER 3

Tapping for Your Ancestors & You

Clearing ancestral and family patterns

The ancestral coping strategies are those things that are passed on to us genetically, emotionally and energetically and we live with them as though they are our own.

There have been experiments, showing that trauma is passed down the family line, through our genes. Mount Sinai Hospital in New York did work with holocaust survivors and proved that the trauma was passed on. Research in Japan gave mice the smell of cherry blossom at the same time as giving them electric shocks, (horrible, I know). When they stopped giving the shocks, the mice still reacted to the smell of cherry blossom as though they were being shocked – and four generations on, new generations of mice were also reacting as though they'd been shocked when they smelt cherry blossom!

It makes sense, doesn't it. If you find something that's dangerous, you want that information to be passed on, to protect the next generations.

Their coping strategies weren't passed on to us to harm us, but with the best of intentions. People pass on whatever they have, even if it isn't working, because it's all that they have.

I like to think of the ancestors passing the "stuff" on, in the hope that someone, somewhere down the line, will draw enough strength from dealing with it that they can let it go on behalf of them all. I see lines of cheering, grateful people when we do this exercise

This exercise allows us to tell the subconscious that we want to clear all the things we've picked up and been carrying, that are not ours.

It's simple and very profound. It can change lives.

Most of the tapping I do, I do on the karate point and I sometimes add in the rest of the points at the end, just because I can! It really doesn't seem to make any difference. I've done whole sessions just using the karate point and sessions where I've added in the other points. Do what feels good to you and if you're not sure of the points, check out the YouTube video, showing the simple way to use EFT.

Also, use your own words for your parents. I've used Mum and Dad and Grandmother. You use whatever you would usually use, so you don't confuse your subconscious. It might be useful to read through the exercise first and make notes on anything that comes up, so that you can decide whether to do the exercise first, or tap on what's come up. As I don't know what your relationship with your family is, I have explanations and suggestions in between the tapping, so reading first and then going back to tap might be easier.

So, here we go....

Tapping on the Karate point

> ***"Even though I have no idea what was going on for my Dad when the sperm that became part of me was formed, I deeply and completely love and accept myself, and maybe even him."***

If loving and accepting Dad is more than you are able to do at this time, then you could do more work on the issues that Dad brings up, before you do this exercise, or add "I'm open to the possibility that at some point in my life, I may consider the possibility of accepting him." Sometimes just a round or two of

> ***"Even though I don't love and accept Dad because he doesn't deserve it and that's the truth,"***

will be enough to make the exercise more comfortable and you can do the same with Mum or Grandmother if it feels necessary.

> ***"Even though I have no idea what was going on for my Mum or my Grandmother when the egg that became part of me was formed, I deeply and completely love and accept myself and maybe even them."***

The egg that became you was created in your mother, when she was created in your grandmother's womb, so whatever was going on for your grandmother at that time will have affected the genes that are switched on for you.

> ***"Even though I have no idea what was going on for my parents when I was conceived, and it's likely that there was a lot, I deeply and completely love and accept us all."***

"It's likely there was a lot," gives the subconscious permission to go in and find whatever there is, even if we have no conscious knowledge of it.

We then move into a conversation with the subconscious, all the while tapping on the karate point.

> ***"Even though, when I was in the womb, I was just a baby, I deeply and completely accept myself."***

> ***"Even though I was just a baby and I was picking up things from my mum and I thought it was all mine, how could I know anything different, I was a baby, feeling those things, I deeply and completely love and accept myself, and maybe even mum."***

> ***"Even though I was just a baby and I was feeling things from my mum, and from my dad through my mum, and from their parents, and their parents' parents right back through time, and I was just a baby and I thought it was all mine, how could I have thought anything different, I deeply and completely accept myself and maybe even all the people who first felt all that "stuff."***

> ***"Even though I thought it was all mine and I've been dutifully carrying it ever since, as though that was the truth, I'd like my subconscious to know that it***

> ***was never mine. I'd like it to clear, now, anything that's not me, anything that's not mine, that I picked up in the womb, or before that, or after that, anything that's not me, anything that's not mine. It's served its purpose and it's finally safe to let it go."***

Top of the head (TOH) : "***It's not mine"***

Eyebrow point (EB) : "***And it never was"***

Side of the eye (SE) : "***And I thought it was"***

Under the eye (UE) : "***Instructing my subconscious to release anything that's not me"***

Under nose (UN) : "***Releasing anything that's not mine***"Chin (CH): "***Allowing it to go"***

Collarbone (CB) : "***Wherever it came from"***

Under arm (UA) : "***Balancing my energy, easily, safely, comfortably and completely because that's what we all deserve."***

I like to do a round of tapping that acknowledges those who came before me in the family line and thank them for what they passed on. We all pass on, unconsciously, what we have. Parts of us will think it's useful, or maybe just don't know what else to do with it. When we do this clearing, the aim is that the healing passes back down the family line and forward through the family line, as well as healing us, that way, the pattern is broken for good, no one has to continue to hold it. If you're in this life right now, tapping on this "stuff," you came to be a pattern breaker and you're doing a great job.

> ***"Even though those who came before me, just passed on what they had, because they didn't know what else to do with it and maybe they hoped that someone, somewhere, could do something with it - and maybe that's me - I deeply and completely love and accept myself and maybe anyone that's involved in this "stuff" in any way. I now release all of this back to the universe, on behalf of anyone involved, for recycling into something more useful, with my thanks for a job well done."***

Notice anything that came up for you as you tapped through this exercise. You could make a note of insights, thoughts or feelings, so you remember to tap on them as necessary.

And now might be a good time to tap on them. There are lots of ways of doing this and remember, some are at the end of the book. One simple way is to just say out loud what you've written in the journal, or what you notice coming up, as you tap, then note anything else that comes up and repeat. Here are some ideas, if it feels necessary and it might not.

> ***"Even though I'm so mad that they passed on their "stuff" to me, I deeply and completely accept myself, whether I accept them or not."***

Another simple way is to focus on the feeling in your body, when you think of what came up. Does that feeling have a colour, a texture, a shape or size? Then that's what you can tap on that and here's an example.

> ***"Even though I have this hard, red knot in my stomach, I deeply and completely accept myself."***

After this exercise give yourself some space. Have a drink, take a few breaths and allow yourself time for things to settle down.

Some people will notice very little during this exercise and it will still be doing its job, others may experience a feeling of relief, sometimes a sense of things falling away, or a lightness. There may be physical feelings too. Everything is normal. It's just your unique way of experiencing things.

This exercise is part of creating a level playing field to work from. When ancestral and family issues are not there it leaves us with our own stuff to deal with and that's far easier.

CHAPTER 4

Rebirthing

Have you ever considered how traumatic going through the birth process must be?

There are all the feelings of the mother to be picked up, all the fear for herself, for the baby. Other people's fears too. Pain and struggle. What a start to life.

Is it surprising that we often hold a belief that life is a struggle? For most of us that's exactly what the beginning of life was, unless you were born by caesarean, in which case there are a whole lot of other issues to work on. And when we're born and we actually come out of the womb, what then? Bright lights, loud noises, being smacked to make us breathe, strange people holding us, passing us around.

It must be terrifying and yet we expect the baby to survive it as it has always been that way. Most of us do, physically, but it may be that there are a lot of emotional issues left to deal with or make sense of.

To clear this is very powerful and it helps to

create the new, level playing field to start our lives from.

If you know of any stories about your birth, that is the place to start from.

That beautiful journal can be useful here too. You could write down any stories you've heard., or just tell yourself the stories that you've heard. If your parents are still alive, you could ask them about your birth. Remember that not all traumas are huge and life threatening, it's the meaning we make of things that happened, that cause the biggest problems for us and being separated from mum, maybe being put into a nursery with other crying babies, will be traumatic to a new born, who suddenly can't hear mum's heartbeat.

It may be that you were breech, or had the cord around your neck, or there was an emergency caesarian, or even, as for some of my clients, that your mother tried to abort you, as in the story in the previous chapter.

You can tap directly on what you know and then you can add things that pop up as "might have beens." You could also use the journal to note any "might have beens" that pop up, if that feels good.

Adding "Maybe" to your tapping on the "might have beens" allows the subconscious to decide if an idea is relevant and use it, without you having to know for sure whether it's a factor. Such as "Even though, maybe, I was terrified when I couldn't hear mum's heartbeat, I'm OK"

There are so many things you could tap on, and the first two sentences below could be used for a breech birth.

> ***"Even though I was the wrong way round, I deeply and completely accept myself."***
>
> ***"Even though I was the wrong way round and maybe I wasn't ready to be born, or maybe I got stuck, I deeply and completely accept myself."***
>
> ***"Even though it was really hard and mum and the nurses and doctors might have been scared, I deeply and completely accept myself."***
>
> ***"Even though it might have felt like I was hurting mum, I'm OK."***
>
> ***"Even though I was scared and I didn't know if either of us would survive, I deeply and completely accept myself."***

> ***"Even though all of that happened and I created vows, decisions and beliefs based on that, I'd like all parts of me to know, that it happened and it's over. I survived and I'm OK and it's finally safe to release all those vows, decisions and beliefs, back to the universe for recycling, into something more useful, with my thanks."***

If you like, you could then tap through the other points, acknowledging what happened and letting go.

For example,

"I was scared"

"It was hard"

"I didn't know what to do"

"And it's over"

"And I'm safe"

"And it's finally"

"Safe to release any trauma or beliefs from that time"

"Back to the universe for recycling, with my thanks."

Then tap on anything else that came up for you. There might be new insights, or new feelings. Don't spend time thinking about it, just go straight in and tap with it. Then do the same again, if more things come up, until it feels clear.

You can do the same with any story about your birth, knowing that there is always likely to have been fear in there and discomfort.

If you had the cord around your neck, it's very likely that you thought you'd die and certain that you'd have felt stuck, pulled, held back, so add those feelings in to the tapping.

Just tell the story as it was, as much as you know, and then deal with the possible feelings and beliefs. You can put in "and maybe I felt," or "and maybe I created beliefs," - you don't have to know for sure. If you put in "maybe," or "perhaps," your subconscious will go in and sort out anything that might match what you've said. It's great at taking a hint and making use of it! I see it as it going through the filing cabinets to find anything that might have any connection to what you're looking at.

Not everyone has a story that they know of, around their birth, but if you do, that's a perfect thing to tap on so that you can clear what you picked up at that time and if you don't have a story, it's good to tap on what's likely to have been there and again, you can use the artfully vague language, while tapping, that allows your subconscious to go in and find whatever's relevant.

For example

> ***"Even though there must have been a lot going on during my birth I deeply and completely love and accept myself"***
>
> ***"Even though, it's likely that my mum was scared and in pain, I deeply and completely love and accept myself"***
>
> ***"Even though I didn't know what was happening and it was uncomfortable and scary and I may have created all sorts of vows, decisions and beliefs based on my birth" I deeply and completely love and accept myself and my mum and everyone else involved, maybe."***

Adding **"maybe,"** gets your rebel on board. If your rebel doesn't want to accept something, it will kick back against what you're doing, if you add "maybe," it's much more likely to be co-operative, as it feels heard.

After dealing with possible stories it can be good

to **imagine what it might have really been like in the womb**, waiting to be born. Think about what might have been going on for the baby that is you and also for your Mum and Dad and maybe even your siblings. What might you all have been feeling or thinking?

It could be good to do some journaling at this point about what might have been going on for all of you, because then it's laid out for you to tap on. Think about your mother's feelings, your feelings, other people's feelings.

This is about using your imagination. What might have been going on? As I said in the previous exercise there was likely to be fear and discomfort at least. What I find with journalling, is that surprising insights often pop up. It's as though you're giving your subconscious a voice.

When you have some ideas about the feelings that might have been there, it's time to tap to clear them.

For Example

> ***"Even though I didn't know what was happening, I deeply and completely love and accept myself."***

> ***"Even though I might have changed my mind about coming into the world, I'm OK."***
>
> ***"Even though it was scary I deeply and completely love and accept myself***
>
> ***"Even though I could feel mum's fear, I'm OK."***
>
> ***"Even though I didn't know if I'd survive, or if mum would, I love and accept us both."***
>
> ***"Even though I was feeling all those things, it happened and it's over and we both survived, and I love and accept myself, the baby that was me and maybe even my mum."***

"It's happened, it's over and I survived," is often new information to some parts of you that are stuck in the original trauma and it can make a huge difference to update them.

When it feels as though you've cleared these it's time to think about **what feelings you would like to have instead**, for the new birth that we're going to create.

Your journal could be useful here too.

Where would you like to be born? Inside? Outside? By water? In the woods? In a meadow?

What feelings would you like to have?

What would you like your Mum to feel?

Do you want your dad to be there? And it's OK if you decide not.

If so, how would you like him to feel?

How would you like the birth to be?

What sort of welcome would you like to have?

Who would you like to be present? If you really can't imagine wanting to be born to your mum, you might choose to be born to someone else, or to have someone there to support your mother so she can support you as you want to be supported, you can even choose to be born to your own higher self. This exercise is about doing it differently rather than replicating the feelings of the original birth.

When you're clear about this, consider next:-

What information would help the baby that is you, to live its life, if it could really know it deep down, for the rest of its life?

There are so many things that it would be helpful to know.

Anything that makes life easier for you, helps you to see yourself, your life, other people in a positive loving way, will help you to create a wonderful life for yourself.

It might be good to take some time to think and maybe journal this before you start tapping. Decide how you'd like the birth to be and who you would like to be there. Get that sorted in your mind first and then start to think about the information you'd like to carry forward with you, for the rest of your life.

What do you wish someone had told you?

How would you like to see yourself?

What would help you to feel safe in your life?

Things such as:-

You are perfect just as you are, humanly perfect and perfectly human.

You are always in the right place at the right time, with the right people, doing the right thing, whatever it looks like on the outside.

You are always loved and loveable, even when

it's not expressed to you, in the way you'd like.

You can only do it right. (Thanks to David Hamilton for that one.)

It's safe to be you.

You are here, at this time, to shine your light in the world.

Your life's purpose is just to be you, in all your multi-coloured glory.

Then, as a final clearing of anything that happened in your first birth, use the notes of what may have happened in your last birth, to tap and clear so you can differentiate between your original birth and the birth you want this time round, e.g.:

> ***"Even though in my first birth, I was frightened, I deeply and completely accept myself."***
>
> ***"Even though I was maybe picking up on my Mum's fear, I deeply and completely accept myself and her."***
>
> ***"Even though she may have been scared I wouldn't survive and maybe she wouldn't either, this birth round I choose us both to know that we survive and the***

> ***birth is easier than we ever thought was possible."***
>
> ***"Even though last time, it was a struggle to be born and I was scared about what I was going into, I'm Ok."***
>
> ***"Even though I may have changed my mind and it was too late, I deeply and completely accept the me that I was then."***
>
> ***"Even though I may have thought that I'd made a mistake, I deeply and completely love and accept myself and my Mum and everyone else involved."***

Continue to tap on anything that comes up for you, about your original birth, until it feels really clear. And of course, if something pops up later, you just go through it again with the new information.

Then, with the **clear idea of the birth** that you would like this time, tap on the experience you're choosing to have this time, including where you fancied being born. Something like:-

> ***"This birth I'm choosing to be born outside, in a meadow, by a lake."***

"I'm choosing my mum to feel safe. To be excited to meet me. I'm choosing for her to feel supported."

"I'm choosing that my dad feels supportive and supported, that he's excited to meet me."

"I choose the baby that's me, to feel safe and loved and supported. Welcomed into the world and curious about being here."

Whatever you thought of, you can tap on.

Then you can add the information you'd like the baby to know, which you've thought of and maybe noted down. Remember some of the examples I suggested earlier in this chapter? You can put them Into tapping statements.

Things such as:-

"I'm choosing the baby that's me, to know deep inside for always, that-

"I am perfect just as I am, humanly perfect and perfectly human."

"I am always in the right place at the right time, with the right people, doing the right thing, whatever it looks like on

the outside."

"I am always loved and loveable, even when it's not expressed to me, in the way I'd like."

"I can only do it right. It's safe to be me."

"I me here at this time, to shine my light in the world."

When you're creating this birth, you can let your Mum know that you will both be safe, you can make the birth as easy and flowing as you like, you can create as much love, cuddling, joy and excitement for yourself as you would like. You can have fireworks and an orchestra if you want! One of my colleagues came out doing the can-can when we did this exercise.

And you can have a sense of joy and delight, anticipation and curiosity about being born into a new life. You can even be there to welcome yourself into the world, as your adult self. This can be particularly important if you find yourself unwilling or unable to see your mother playing a loving role. You can also invite other people that you think will support you, to be there. You can invite angels, guides, whatever you can imagine, you can create.

When you've tapped on all your notes and you feel ready,

Close your eyes and imagine being that baby, ready to be born, curled up warm and comfy in the womb, with the birth canal open wide, so you can see the light at the end of the tunnel. Go through the whole birth, while you tap the karate point, until you've been successfully born and received the loving welcome you chose.

Very occasionally people find it difficult to create the birth as they want it, and this means that there's more tapping to do.

Often, it's because it feels as though the people at the birth won't be able to do what you want them to do, in which case choose someone else who can do that for you, and it might even be your adult self. It could also be because you are afraid of what life will be like for you, in which case, consider what the fears are and tap to clear them, and then rebirth yourself again.

Don't continue to try the rebirth if it's not as you want it, clear what is going on for you first, so that when you rebirth, it's easy and joyful. Remember, this isn't a test, it's not pass or fail, it's a process of discovery

If you're happy with how the birth went, tap on

> ***"Even though the first birth was as it was, I'd like all parts of me to know that this new birth is the one to refer to from now on, unless I do another rebirth, because this is the beginning of the rest of my life."***

Then take some time and a drink of water, to allow the changes to integrate.

The subconscious doesn't know the difference between reality and imagination, so this exercise will re-programme it, give it a different starting place to refer to, as it checks back to see what it should be thinking about what is going on in your life at this moment, and therefore your life and your beliefs are likely to be different. It can have a huge impact on you and how you live your life, and the results are often seen later, as you look back and see how you've been doing things differently.

You can give yourself time to allow this to integrate and move on to the other exercises after a few days, when you feel balanced and comfortable.

I do this work in the initial session with each client and usually wait for 2 weeks for the next session, so that the change has been integrated and the client has a clearer idea of what has changed, what's the same and if there is anything going on for them which they hadn't noticed before. You can do that, or move right on, whatever feels good to you.

CHAPTER 5

Past Lives

It doesn't matter whether you believe that we've lived other lives, or not. The concept can be a great way to get to deep "stuff" and heal it.

Whether we choose to see past lives as lives that we have lived in a previous time, or as connecting energetically in the Field, or Matrix, to lives that others have lived, or as our subconscious' way of creating a metaphor for us to work with, past life work can have a big impact.

On a scientific level, Bruce Lipton, in "Biology of Belief," talks about the membrane around the cell acting as its brain. It responds to environmental signals. On the surface of our cells are identity receptors, which download the signal that is us, from the Universe, or the Matrix.

When people have organ transplants, it has been seen that they can change quite significantly. A vegetarian can find themselves fancying a hamburger! This may be because when we have someone else's organ live in our body, we're downloading two different signals, ours and the organ donors. You can see that it might get confusing.

The self-receptors on the cell membrane read a signal of SELF coming from the external environment. It's rather like a television set receiving a signal. One day the set may blow and we can't receive the signal. If we get a new set, and tune in again, we pick up the signal again. The death of the TV didn't affect the broadcast. If, after we die, someone is born who downloads the same signal as we are doing now, we're back in the world, reborn. And maybe this is reincarnation. And whatever you believe is perfect for you right now and you can still use the concept of past lives to do healing, whatever you believe.

Three cases that have had the most profound effect of any that I've worked with were three people who independently and at different times came to me and said that their issues had roots back to the time of Atlantis. Past lives are not something I routinely bring up with clients I don't know, and they brought it up themselves, one in the first session and another when they had worked with me and felt comfortable with me.

Interestingly they each told the same story, of powerlessness and betrayal, but from the perspectives of their life at the time. One was looking after animals and felt that she'd let them down when she couldn't save them in the cataclysm that ended Atlantis. In this life, she refused to connect to humans, she would only talk to and connect to animals. She made sure she couldn't see or hear anybody and life was very difficult for her.

One of the other clients had been looking after children and again, there was the sense of betrayal and powerlessness as she hadn't been able to save the children. In this life, she was finding herself over protective of the children in her family

The third person was me! I'd had a memory for a long time, ever since I could remember, of standing on land, in front of a river or canal, looking up at someone on a bridge above me, feeling as though my heart would break. There was a huge sense of betrayal and I was saying "but you told me...." Just as everything fell to pieces around us. As I explored the memory and the feelings, what felt true to me, was that I'd been used to keep the populace calm. I'd been told that all was well, there were no problems and in good faith, I'd passed that message on and it was a lie, although I had no way of knowing that at the time. So, for me, there was the sense of others betraying me and also, the sense that I'd betrayed others, however unwittingly. There was a sense that I "should" have known, I "should" have seen what was happening, I "should" have been able to keep things safe. You can see where my habit of "shoulding" on myself may have started.

The clients and I treated their memories as though they were specific events in this lifetime and cleared them by tapping. We cleared the trauma they'd experienced and stored, the feelings they were still carrying and all the vows, decisions and beliefs they had created because of this event. In each case the whole belief system of the client changed and in one case, perfect eyesight was restored, although after 3 weeks it began to change again as new issues came to the surface.

As for me, I found it really helpful in clearing all sorts of layers of feelings and beliefs and I learnt to be kinder to myself.

Another time that past lives came up in a big way, which I still remember with amazement, was when I was running a retreat in Slovenija. Slovenija has a very active tapping community, thanks to Pika Rajner, who invited me to run retreats at Lake Bled. Those retreats have been real highlights in my life, allowing me to help people to get deep into what's going on for them and to facilitate huge change.

In this particular retreat, I was working with one of the participants when she suddenly said, "This has a past life root." We explored what was going on and she said she'd been killed in a battle. We cleared the trauma and the beliefs and as the retreat progressed, 2 other people also connected to past lives with huge trauma. Amazingly, it turned out they were all part of the same battle. There was the person who'd been killed, the person who'd killed him and the wife of the person who'd been killed. Not only that, they'd chosen to sit next to each other! There was a lot of deep healing done in that retreat!

One thing I've found when working with clients is, as we work on an issue, be that a belief, or a feeling, they may experience a feeling in their body. It may be a pain in a particular place, or a sensation in their body that reminds them of other times and places. It could feel like a stab in the back, a weight on their shoulders, a lump in their throat and it's easy to clear any link with past lives, "just in case". Sometimes you may get an intuition that this may be from another time, another life, so be brave. It's easy to throw that in as a possibility, so it can be cleared, without having to go in and explore a specific past life. My experience is that those feelings often link to multiple past lives, so acknowledging that may be where they come from and clearing them, can be a short cut to huge and profound healing.

One really simple way to do this is as you're tapping on whatever's come up, for you or for the client, you can add

> ***"And even though that may come from another time, life, or dimension, I choose to release it now. This is ---- (this year's date) and whatever happened, happened. It's over and I've survived. I no longer need to carry this with me. I release it with love, back to the universe for recycling."***

When releasing long held things, whether that be beliefs or feelings, rather than fighting them or rejecting them, which can lead to them fighting back, it can be useful to acknowledge the place they've had in your life and then return them to the universe for recycling into something more useful, or return them to the universe with your love and thanks.

Something like,

> ***"Even though I've had this for such a long time, I now release it back to the universe for recycling into something more useful, with my love and thanks for a job well done."***

The truth is, whatever part was creating the feelings or beliefs was absolutely doing the best for you that it could, with the knowledge and information it had, when it started doing that. Releasing it with love is the equivalent of acknowledging its sterling work and giving it a retirement gold clock for a job well done. Honour is satisfied, everyone's happy and it now becomes possible to do something else instead.

If you have past life memories yourself, you could **write them down in your journal, or just talk about them to yourself, or to someone else.**

Now you can tap on them as though they were events in this life, scale the feelings around them, use the Colour and Shape technique to bundle the emotions and tap, which will mean that you won't have to re-experience any trauma. ** More information on the Colour and Shape Technique can be found in the Appendix.*

"Even though when I was in that life, this happened and I felt like this, (Put in your own specific events and feelings) that was then, and this is now"

"Even though that's how it was, I survived, and I'm ok, and I no longer need to carry that old trauma, and I deeply and completely love and accept myself and the me I was then."

"Even though the beliefs, vows and coping strategies that I created then got me here, I'm here now, and it's finally ok to release the need to hold on to all that old "stuff", and release it all back to the universe for recycling into something more useful, with my thanks for a job well done.".

Then tap around the points, using some of the words as reminder phrases.

Another useful phrase, that updates the subconscious which is often running on old, outdated information, is to remind it that

"What happened, happened and it's over. I survived and it's finally safe to let it go. It's (whatever year it is now) and I no longer need that."

Essentially you are telling the subconscious to hold anything that's been useful and given you resources, and to let go of anything that's not working/unhelpful/unhealthy. It's back to updating the computer that's your subconscious, with new information. You can then check in to see if any other thoughts, feelings or memories have come up and if so, you can tap to clear them. If nothing more comes up, you can move on.

If you don't have past life memories, you could do a general tap to instruct your subconscious to clear anything that you're holding from previous lives, even if you don't know what it is.

For example:-

> ***"Even though, I may be holding on to old beliefs, feelings and vows, from other lives, times and dimensions, that was then and this is now. I'm here now, with all the resources I have, and it's finally ok to release anything from those times that no longer serves me, while keeping the resources I gained, and I deeply and completely love and accept all parts of me."***
>
> ***"Even though there may be things from other lives, times or dimensions that are***

influencing me now, that was then and this is now, and it's ok to let them go now."

"Even though I've held onto all that stuff for all this time and it's served a useful purpose in the past, that time is over and it's ok to let it go."

"Even though it's served a useful purpose, I choose to keep the strengths and the learnings that it's given me and release all the old rubbish, and I deeply and completely accept myself and anyone who may have been involved."

And again, tap around the points, using some of the words as reminder phrases. Remember you are telling the subconscious to hold anything that's been useful and to let go of anything that's not working/unhelpful/unhealthy. You could then check if anything else has come up and then tap to clear that. If nothing came up, it's time to move on.

Now that you have an idea of what's not really yours and what is and you've done some letting go, how does that feel?

Is there an emptiness where all that stuff was? Does it feel scary to be without it? Or does it feel beautifully clear and clean?

If it feels uncomfortable in any way, that's the time to tap on those uncomfortable feelings and you can easily do that with the Colour and shape tapping, or just by tapping and talking to yourself about what you're feeling.

> ***"Even though it feels so strange not holding onto all that stuff and I don't know if I like it, or if it's safe to not hold it, I deeply and completely love and accept myself anyway."***
>
> ***"Even though I feel empty without it I deeply and completely love and accept myself anyway."***
>
> ***"Even though it feels disloyal to let it go, it I'm open to the possibility that I'm letting go on behalf of those who couldn't let go themselves. I validate all that they went through and now I'm freeing all of us from the need to continue this pattern, and I deeply and completely love and accept myself and them."***

Sometimes we can find ourselves holding onto to things out of loyalty to those who experienced them before we did. I was recording a DVD with a colleague who had a Jewish family background and eventually we got to the point where she discovered that she wasn't releasing the things that stopped her being happy, because being happy would be disloyal to those in her family who had lived miserable lives. That took quite a bit of negotiating with Parts, to get them to agree to release the old beliefs, so it can be useful to check if there's any feelings of disloyalty when you're creating a different life for yourself.

You can also focus on how any discomfort feels in the body and clear it that way.

> ***"Even though I can feel a hole where all that "stuff" was and it feels uncomfortable, I deeply and completely accept myself."***

> ***"Even though it feels a bit empty, I now choose to fill it with this colour."***

At this point imagine if you could fill that hole with a colour, what would it be? Don't get hooked on choosing the "right" colour, if in doubt, go for rainbow and then imagine breathing in that colour, through your crown chakra, at the top of your head, allowing it to flood through your body, into every cell, clearing all damage, all toxins, anything not needed on your journey, filling you up, spilling over, washing through your energy system, filling and expanding your aura, helping your

chakras to clean and spin as they are intended. Enjoy that until it feels you've done enough. You can do this as often as you choose. It can be a quick way to get back into balance and give yourself a boost.

Sometimes it may need time for the neural pathways to readjust, for the old ones that supported the old behaviour and beliefs to fade and the new ones that support your new way of being to grow and strengthen and you can tap directly on that.

> ***"Even though I have those old neural pathways that supported me in the old patterns, I'd like them to know they've done a great job and that job is now complete, and it's ok for them to fade and allow new neural pathways to grow to support the new behaviour, and I deeply and completely love and accept myself and them."***

You can also tap on feeling discombobulated! - I love that word!

> ***"Even though I'm so tired and my energy is scrambled, I choose my energy to balance easily, safely and comfortably and I deeply and completely love and accept myself and all parts of me."***

You can also have a good drink of water and a sleep

You can tap on whatever thoughts or feelings come up until it feels comfortable to no longer carry all that stuff that's not really yours. Give yourself time for these changes to integrate and that might be a couple of weeks. You'll know when it feels right to look at the next layer of "stuff,'" which is to l**ook at your own past** and the **beliefs and vows and decisions** you've made based on what you've done and not done, and what's happened to you over your life.

Chapter 6

Our Own Past

You can only do it right.

There are no mistakes, you haven't messed up, you're not in trouble, all is as you planned it.

"They" may have told you, that you "got it wrong," you "shouldn't have done it that way." They have their opinions, based on someone else's opinions, based on someone else's opinions, based on what was going on in that life, maybe hundreds of years ago.

Parts of you know better. Deep within you is the Part of you that knows exactly who you are and why you're here.

It remembers what a treat it felt to be coming back to a physical earth again, to try out new things, new ways of being, new thoughts.

Can you remember the excitement? The good wishes of those around you?

Can you remember what a great idea it seemed and how you knew that throughout your life, you'd attract other souls who would show you who you really are? Sometimes by showing you who you aren't.

I always think that those who create the most problems for us must love us very much to have volunteered for such a rubbish job. It helps me to think that, anyway!

Your past is your past. Except that **while you're still holding emotions and beliefs based on the past, it's really your present,** because those things are influencing you every moment of your day, whether you realise it or not.

And it's not the things that happen to us that are the problem, it's the meanings and beliefs that we make from them.

The meanings about ourselves, about others, about the world and everything in it.

We've looked at how other people's past has impacted on us and now what about our own past?

What have you done, or not done in the past that you've regretted?

What have people said to you, or you've said to you, that still hurts?

Who are you blaming? "Them" or yourself, or the whole world?

What is in your past that still has emotional power over you?

If thinking of a person or an event creates a bodily feeling that's uncomfortable, then it is still influencing your life right now.

Releasing that feeling doesn't mean that you're condoning what happened, what someone did, it's about giving yourself permission not to have to drag those people and the beliefs and feelings you created, with you for the rest of your life.

In setting others free, from the role we gave them so long ago, we're actually, setting ourselves free to be ourselves and wouldn't that be good? For ourselves and the rest of the world.

Sometimes people talk about Karma as though it's a punishment and something that you have to suffer through because of misdeeds in the past.

What if it's really, about experiencing the other side of the coin, the opposite to what you experienced in your last life, and when you've done that and can make new decisions, it is alright to let go of whatever the lesson is? Wouldn't that make sense?

Once a child has learnt to spell a particular word easily, you wouldn't expect them to continue learning that same word forever, would you? You'd expect them to learn something else that they don't know.

That's what life's like. You learn and then you move on to learning something else. It's not about punishment, it's about learning, and once you've learnt, you are free to move on.

Of course, you don't have to, you can stay and relearn, and relearn for the rest of your life if you choose - I've done that a lot! It's important though to recognise that that's what it is, a choice and that you can make other choices as soon as you choose to.

And of course, it would be lovely to tap on any uncomfortable feelings that pop up at the thought of that being true.

We all have our stories and we stick to them. Sometimes we use them as justification for staying stuck.

It can feel so much easier to blame a parent for

what they did and said than to admit that part of you is scared to make changes. In the West, certainly, we're very good at blame. Things "have to" be someone's fault, so rather than blaming me, I'll blame you.

And of course, that leaves us in the stuck, powerless place, where we can't do anything different because we've given our power away.

How would it feel to you, if you believed that you were responsible for your life and what happens in it? Does it feel uncomfortable?

Would you like to tap on it?

"Even though I don't like that idea, I'm Ok."

"Even though it makes me angry just to think about it, I feel as though I'm being blamed, I'm OK."

"Even though I was told that it's got to be someone's fault and if it's not theirs it must be mine, I'm open to the possibility that there is no fault here; it's what happened because of the beliefs I've been carrying, or they were carrying and it's finally safe to release those beliefs along with all the pain and trauma that they caused, so that I can create a new and different and nurturing life for myself. It's

what I deserve and it's what I came here to do, whether I remember it or not."

So .....

What and who has been, or still is, in your life that you're holding on to even when it doesn't feel good?

What event comes back to haunt you?

Who do you keep thinking of, even though they're no longer in your life?

What words do you find yourself repeating?

What conversations do you rerun?

What things have been said to you?

What things have been done to you?

Take some time to think. You might want to do a brainstorm in your journal and write down whatever comes up, so you know what would be useful to tap on, or just think your way through.

And I'd like to say here and now, that if you're dealing with major trauma, or abuse of any kind you might want to find a skilled EFT therapist to do this work with, because you'll find it

easier and it will feel safer. Your subconscious will have been trying to protect you from those things all your life, so it won't want you to go in and start undoing its hard work, which makes clearing things more difficult. With a good therapist that you connect well with it will be easier and quicker and less uncomfortable to make changes.

If you're tapping with yourself, think of the answers to those questions and check where you're feeling the feelings and then tap on them using the "The Colour and Shape Technique," page 137 , **EFT and Timelines**, or **"Talking and Tapping."** There will be layers that come up as you clear and you may well discover things that you didn't realise you believed, or are holding on to. This is a great gift and all you do is keep tapping as the layers come up, until you feel that you've come to a comfortable place to pause.

If at any time, you feel overwhelmed and there's too much to clear in the time you have, you can use something I created way back at the beginning of my time using EFT, when I was less skilled and it took me longer to clear things. I called it the Box Technique (and you'll find it in the techniques section page 143) and it's a great way to store unfinished business safely. I love it when I hear people presenting

at a conference suggesting it, without any idea where it came from. It feels so right that once things have been created, they are available for anyone to use. To see my work spreading like the ripples in a pond is very satisfying and of course, I'm hoping that what I share here will do the same. It feels as though, in my own quiet way, I've done what I came for.

Tap as you read the next part, if you're not tapping already.

Remember, however painful, those things are, they are not you. They are things that happened to you, and who you are right now, with all the understanding and resources you have, is because of them, both the people and the events. That was their purpose. To give you the strength you needed to complete your life as yourself. Expressing the divine spark of the universe that you are. Whenever you are ready to do that, you can let the crap go. It will have served its purpose.

Sometimes we hold onto our wounds because no one has acknowledged them, certainly not the people who wounded us and the truth is, often, they won't do that, they don't have the conscious understanding and if that's what you're waiting for, you may be waiting for the rest of your life.

Those people weren't operating from a logical adult space, they were operating from a small child, hurt space, as were the people who hurt them.

Letting go of the wounds they've given you, is your adult saying to your child, you're safe now, I can look after you. You are releasing yourself from having to drag those people with you for the rest of your life. The contract between you is complete and it's time to move on and create the life you really want, where you get to live as yourself, the authentic self that was hiding beneath the layers of tarnish that it acquired during all those events.

It's saying that those people and events have completed their job and they no longer deserve this importance in your life.

You can even chat to your Inner Child while you're tapping and acknowledge what they went through. You can tell them how brave they were and how proud of them you are, how much you love them. Let them know that you are with them and they don't have to do this on their own anymore.

You can do this tapping all in one go, or take

some time. There's no right way, just the way that's right for you. Sometimes just tapping on the emotions until some of the intensity is reduced is the best starting point and then you can look at the other options; sometimes it might feel good to go straight to talking to the Child. Trust yourself. Whatever feels right to you will be right and you can do it again, differently, later, if that feels right. Listen to yourself. If you're angry, rant while you tap, if sadness comes up, tap. If it's hurt, tap. If there's something you want to say to someone who hurt you, say it while you tap. It's all good and it all works, and if it's not working, it just means there's a small child inside holding on because they think if they let go, they're letting go of who they are; they're afraid, so go in and find that child and reassure them. Let them know that they are not what happened. They are always themselves and you can keep them safe now.

I will offer some possibilities for tapping below. If they feel useful, use them and then add your own thoughts and feelings. What comes up for you as an individual, is always going to be the most on target. Remember, you can only do it right. The worst that can happen is nothing happens. And you'll always get information that will be useful to tap on.

"Even though it wasn't fair, and that's the truth, I love and accept myself, whether I accept them or not."

"Even though they really hurt me and they never said they were sorry, I love and accept the me that experienced that."

"Even though sometimes it feels like it ruined my life, I'm open to the possibility that it gave me the wisdom and the strength and the understanding that I have right now."

"Even though I don't want to let any of this go, it feels like I'm letting them off the hook, I choose to recognise that I'm the one getting off the hook and maybe they don't deserve to have me drag them with me for the rest of my life."

"Even though this is my story, and I'm sticking to it, I love and accept myself and the Parts of me that want to hold on."

"Even though I can't let it go and I don't want to let it go and you can't make me – and that's the truth – I'm open to the possibility that I can hold onto this as long as I want and I can let it go

whenever I want. It's always my choice and that's OK."

"Even though the scared child inside me doesn't feel safe, I'd like all my young Parts to know that they're ok. They did a great job, in the only way they could, and I love and accept them exactly as they are. No one's in trouble, we're all safe. Now it's time for my adult to keep them safe, they've done their job and now it's ok for them to go and play, or have a nap, and I love and accept them all."

Remember if you're uncomfortable with any of this, find an experienced therapist that you can really connect to and do the work with them. It will make it quicker and easier

When you've cleared the emotion linked to those events and those people then it's time to look at the beliefs, vows and decisions you made based on them, because it's those that are running the show. It's never what happened to us that causes the problem, it's the beliefs we make about ourselves and others and the world, based on what happened, that causes us the problem.

CHAPTER 7

Beliefs

- **Your beliefs become your thoughts**
- **Your thoughts become your words**
- **Your words become your actions**
- **Your actions become your habits**
- **Your habits become your values**
- **Your values become your destiny**

Gandhi

You can see how that happens.

If you create a belief and that's what you think about, you'll talk about it all the time, you can't help yourself. We all give ourselves away with our language.

"Mustn't be greedy,"

"Who do they think they are?"

"I can't do…,"

"I'm not very good at….,"

"Things never work out for me,"

"Just my luck." And all the rest of it!

Then you start to act as though it's true and things don't work out for you.

What do you do to make sure that's the truth? **Because that's what we do**. The subconscious sees what it expects to see and if there's not a match, **it will delete or distort what you see until it matches your expectations**. And we all do it in different ways.

A client was having a hard time at university. She decided that she was going to leave and go home as she wasn't any good at what she did, everyone else was better than her, she'd never be successful. Then she mentioned that she'd won a competition to design a logo for the town that the university was in.

When questioned about that and it not matching the belief she was no good, she said, "It was only a logo, it only took 10 minutes and everyone is better than me at everything else!" She won the only two competitions during her time at university, but managed to keep her beliefs intact, because that's what we do: hang on to our beliefs whether they're helpful or not! The subconscious sees what it expects to see.

That's when we create our values. If something happens consistently then we assume it's for the best. We create our values around it.

If your belief is, "I can't be successful," you won't do anything that would allow that belief to be challenged and allow you to be successful; or you'll do something that might take you towards success and then you'll sabotage yourself. You'll create values that match your belief and will support it, such as **"it's more spiritual to be humble." "Blessed are the meek".**

And then that becomes your destiny. If thoughts, words, actions, values, habits are all aligned, you ARE creating your destiny. How could you create anything else from all of this? You are vibrating at the level that will attract what you are expecting. If this idea is new to you, explore the **Law of Attraction**. More details are in the bibliography at the end of the book. page 148.

What stories do you tell yourself?

What stories do you tell other people?

When do you use the word "always"? As in "I always get it wrong," "That always happens to me."

When do you use the word never? As in "I

never get what I want." "It never happens for me." "I'll never be that lucky."

Those statements are showing you your beliefs and what you believe is what you create in your life.

Those are all great places to start.

It could be time for some more journalling, or talking and then tapping.

You could ask yourself questions.

Where might those beliefs have come from?

Who might they have come from?

Where have you acted those beliefs out?

If there was a deeper belief, supporting that one, what might it be?

Who else had that belief?

These are all questions that will bring up more information to be tapped on. Often, it's by tapping on one belief that a major belief underpinning everything else comes to light, so celebrate when it does.

You could ask yourself what things were said to you as a child. What were the family sayings?

"Things like **"money doesn't grow on trees,"** or **"you can't have everything you want,"** do not help you to be abundant, in fact the opposite is the case.

Some tapping ideas.

> ***"Even though I always tell myself .... I deeply and completely accept myself anyway."***

Keep tapping on the layers that come up as you tap, with the feelings tapping, or talk and tap.

> ***"Even though I always tell other people .... I deeply and completely accept myself anyway."***

Keep tapping on the layers that come up as you tap, with the body tapping, or talk and tap.

Then tap on the things you say to yourself, the always things and the never things.

And for all of that work, you can add in,

> ***"Even though those things happened and I did all of that, I'd like every part of me to know, that whatever happened to create that, those things happened and they're over and I've survived, and it's now finally safe for me to let all of this go.***

I can keep whatever's useful and release whatever is no longer for my highest good with my thanks to the parts that worked so hard to keep me safe in their way".

"Even though I have all these unhelpful beliefs I choose to release them now."

"Even though I made so many vows and decisions and beliefs based on all those things, I just didn't have enough information then and I have new information now and I choose to release those vows, decisions and beliefs on behalf of all of us. "

And of course, when you've had those beliefs for so long a part of you might be worried about who you'll be without them, so you can tap on any identity issues that come up.

"Even though I've had those beliefs for so long that I won't know who I am without them, I'm Ok. "

"Even though I won't know who I am, or how to be and what to do, I'm so glad that there's a Part of me that already does know and I ask it to share that information with all the other parts of me."

> ***"Even though I won't know who I am without those beliefs, maybe I'll just be me without these beliefs, no more and no less."***

People often think if they change something like a feeling or belief they have to change all sorts of things in their life, but that isn't true. They could continue life exactly as it is now, but it would be a choice, not a "have to." And that means they can do something different whenever it feels good to them, they're never stuck.

After you've cleared all that you can find, check back to a time when those beliefs would have been in play. How does that situation feel now? Check a time in the future when those beliefs would have been running the show. You may, or may not need to do some tapping on specific events of those times.

CHAPTER 8

The Past is the Past

***"You are here to enable the divine purpose of the Universe to unfold. That is how important you are."* Ekhart Tolle**

Ask yourself,

"If it was true that the past is the past, what would be different for me now?"

"What happens when I think of starting my life again without all of that "stuff?"

Notice what comes up for you, whether it feels new and exciting and possible, or totally impossible, or anything in between.

If it doesn't feel possible and good, try asking yourself some more questions.

"Who am I holding myself back for?"

"Who won't I let go of until they've apologised?"

"What would I have to forgive myself for to let go?"

"What would I have to forgive "them" for, to let go?"

"What part of me is frightened to do it differently and why?"

You could write down your answers in your journal and be honest, there is no one to fool but yourself. And all you're doing is clearing out the layers. When you can see all of this as just information, rather than a judgement on yourself, things flow so much more easily.

Notice what feelings come when you consider each question. Are there fears or uncomfortable feelings, or is there a sense of excitement and anticipation when you consider doing things differently?

Is there a sense of holding onto the old until.....?

When you have some information about these things, you'll have found what can be tapped on.

Track the feelings that are in your body, when you think of the answers to one of the questions above. You could tap directly on those feelings, or it may be possible to use those feelings to track back to an early childhood time when you had them and tap on the feelings around that event.

You could talk to the part of you that first felt those feelings and explain that that was then and this is now.

Or you could just talk out the answers while you tap. Whatever works for you is what works and if it's not working, remember, it just means there's a small child part inside you that's frightened, that you haven't met yet. Go in and introduce yourself. Do it gently, they may be frightened and hiding. You could even tap on,

> ***"Even though you're frightened and hiding and don't believe you're safe, I'm here to take care of you. You've been very brave and now it's my turn to look after you."***

> ***"Even though little.... (your name) felt all those feelings then and didn't know what to do with them, that was then and this is now, we've survived and maybe I could help little..... to let go of those feelings now, because I have more resources than she/he had then and we're both OK either way."***

You can talk to the Subconscious, negotiate with the parts that aren't happy,

> ***"Even though part of me doesn't want to***

> ***let "them" off the hook, maybe it would be OK to release the need to hold onto those old feelings, because maybe they don't deserve that amount of importance in my life."***

You could ask the Subconscious to let old neural pathways go and create new neural pathways that will support the new way of being.

> ***"Even though those old neural pathways have supported the old behaviour so well, I'm doing things differently now and I instruct my Subconscious to allow the old neural pathways to fade away safely and to create new neural pathways that support the new ways of feeling and being, in a safe, healthy way."***

Whatever pops into your head is what to tap on. Remember, you can only do it right

Restoring ourselves to factory settings

You can remind yourself that this is like **restoring your computer back to factory settings,** before all the rubbish was downloaded. You know what I mean! This is about rediscovering yourself, reconnecting with the core of who you are. All the information that you need to do that, is available to you right here and now.

Life is like the dance of the universe, with flow in and out. It's about making joyful decisions, living in bliss. Love is the key.

Gregg Braden talks about the survival of the most loving. When every human being recognizes every other human being as an individual frequency of the white light of the universe, the white light will return.

As more and more people return to who they are, to all that they are, we reach the critical mass where the tipping point comes.

You ***can*** live it and others can model that or not. You ***can*** show that it's possible, but it's not your job to do it for anyone else, or to decide that that is what they need to do.

When you've cleared what you can find that's uncomfortable, still using your emotions as your guide, think of someone close to you, open your heart and feel love - how does that feel? If you think of people in your past, open your heart and feel love - how does that feel?

Tap on anything that isn't love, they are just more layers that you didn't spot earlier because they were covered by bigger layers.

When you can feel the love, when you're feeling comfortable with the past, check again where we started this chapter.

If the past really was the past, how would that be? Here and now with all the strength and wisdom you've gained?

If you were starting life again with the wisdom you've learned how does it feel? How would things be different? How would you be different? How would the world be different? Try brainstorming and see what comes up. Check out the feelings around what you brainstormed. If anything feels uncomfortable, or you can hear yourself telling yourself things that aren't helpful, you have your next layer of tapping.

You can try any of these statements to tap on, if they seem appropriate.

> ***"Even though different feels scary and it gives me this feeling, I deeply and completely accept myself."***
>
> ***"Even though I won't know who I am if I do things differently, I'm OK and I'm open to the possibility that I'm always me, whatever I do or don't do."***
>
> ***"Even though I don't know how to be***

in the world when I'm seeing things differently, there's a part of me that already knows how to do that and I'd like it to share the information with the rest of me, with my thanks."

When it feels as though you're comfortable when you consider changes, think of yourself, open your heart and feel love. Really imagine living the changes.

Check how that feels now. If there is more to do, do it. If it feels exciting, if you have a sense of curiosity, then you are ready to move forward to **"Designing your Future."**

CHAPTER 9

Designing Your Future

When we think of our future and how we want it to be, we are often our own worst enemies. It can be when every limiting belief we have shows up and tries to run the show.

All those determined voices that we've heard for so much of our life, from others initially, and later on, the chances are, that we took over the job and said those unhelpful things to ourselves!

How often have you said to yourself things like:-

"That's never going to happen for me."

"It's alright for them."

"I won't be that lucky."

"It'll be too hard."

"I was never meant to be rich."

"People don't like you if you're ......successful/ rich/happy or a million other things."

"Rich men are bastards."

"I'd rather be poor and happy." (As though if you're going to be happy, the rules say you also have to be poor! And there will be parts of us that absolutely do believe that these are the rules.)

"I don't know how."

"It'll take too long."

And 2 of my childhood favourites –

"Money doesn't grow on trees, you know!"

"You can't have everything, you know."

There is something about the "you know," on the end that makes it seems like THE truth, THE reality, something that you "should" have known.

And you'll have multiple sayings all your own.

And these didn't start with you. You got them from your parents and maybe your grandparents, who got them from their parents and it goes right back through time. Maybe someone, hundreds of years ago came up with them because they fitted what was going on around them and maybe it even seemed some sort of consolation. Some of the voices definitely come from others religious backgrounds.

"Blessed are the meek."

"It's easier for a camel to go through the eye of a needle, than for a rich man to get into heaven."

When I was working on my money beliefs several years ago, I had a sudden flashback to being in Sunday school at about age seven, when we were told that saying. I remembered clearly thinking I'd better never be rich then, as it sounds as though it's important to get into heaven! And guess what, I'd spent my life trying really hard not to be rich and succeeding beautifully!

When I had a very successful EFT business I managed to sabotage it regularly. I remember one time, looking at what was in the bank and looking at the clients who were already booked in and part of me wanted to celebrate and the part that believed everything my dad ever said to me, believed that it wasn't safe to say things were going well, **"The gods won't be mocked and they'll take it away."** I heard myself say, **"This won't last."** And amazingly there was some comfort in that. A bit like putting on well-worn shoes. They may not support you well, but your feet recognise them and they feel right.

After I'd said, **"This won't last,"** the phone

stopped ringing immediately, and it took me two weeks of tapping to get back to where I had been before. Not only that, I did the same thing three times and as a final go, my business phone number, which was on my website and all my stationery, was accidently cancelled and the phone company said I couldn't have it back!! That took some serious tapping, I can tell you. I rang the phone company every day and it wasn't until I felt emotionally OK, whatever the outcome, that I found a wonderful woman at the phone company, whose boyfriend worked in the number distribution centre and she persuaded him to give me my number back. This was before mobiles were the main source of connection, of course.

I find it really empowering, recognising if things aren't working, there's something in the way, and it's something I can do something about. I've proved the truth of that for myself, so many times in my life. And of course, I've helped many clients to see the reality of that too.

When your belief is that things happen to you randomly, it's really disempowering. It means that there's no point in making changes, because something else random might hit you. It leaves us in a position where we start looking for who, or what to blame and once we do that, we've lost our ability to make changes. Often society and our family will have taught us that if something goes wrong, it has to be someone's fault and as we don't want it to be ours, we look "out there," for where to point the finger of blame.

Just think how much more helpful it might be, if we could acknowledge that some belief that we're running, might have helped us to attract that into our lives. If that was so, we have power to find the belief and change it for something more useful for us, at this point in our life. That's the way we can begin to design the life that we really want to live, for ourselves.

It's interesting when we come to thinking about creating the life that we want, because it's not only the old beliefs that get in the way, it's other people, or rather our beliefs about other people. It really is our beliefs that run the show for us.

When we consider our dream life we often then think of other people and how they might fit into our dream and we can then have a tendency, to stop ourselves dreaming, in case others don't like it, or they get hurt, or angry. In case we get into trouble. It goes back to childhood, when we might have tried to share our dreams with those around us and had them crushed by others' versions of reality.

We can also stop ourselves dreaming for the fear of our disappointment, if the dreams don't manifest as we want. Actually, other people will often crush our dreams because they believe they'll save us the disappointment of them not working out. Many really limiting beliefs were passed on with the best of intentions.

I'd like you to join me in an exercise to help you to get clear about what life you'd like to manifest for yourself.

First thing, take a moment to set your intention for what we're about to do.

There are many ways to make changes; you can do it easily, joyfully, happily, or with a struggle. It could be difficult, painful, or successful. Which do you choose? And if there's a voice saying it can't be done easily, or you don't deserve to do it happily, then you know what your next tapping will be, along with any beliefs that popped up as you read the first part of this chapter.

Call in help. Ask your guides, your angels, your higher self, the universe to be with you and support you in what you are doing.

The first thing is to consider your goals. What would you like to call into your life? What

would you like your life to look like?

If you had a magic wand.

If you could wave it and **you didn't have to consider anyone else** at all and you **didn't have to know how things could happen**, where would you be in five years time and what would you be doing?

Think about your life in five years time.

What would you like it to look like?

Where would you like to be?

Who would you like to be with?

Who would you like in your life?

What will you be doing?

How will you be feeling?

Don't forget, we're talking **magic wand** here.

I suggest 5 years and the magic wand because if I say next year, as soon as you start to imagine, a part of you will go, "How's that going to happen by next year then!" and it stops you in your tracks. You cut yourself down to a smaller more manageable size, so you don't get disappointed.

This exercise is about being gloriously, amazingly out there. It's about imagining all those things that you haven't even allowed yourself to consider as possible for you.

It's getting clear about what things would feel great for you if you only had yourself to consider and the angels could fix it, (and of course they can if you ask and then allow them).

The aim of this exercise is to get a clear idea of what you'd really like, what lights your fire, so that the universe can use that information to attract it to you. Without the clarity, you could be attracting all sorts of things and often things that you don't really want.

The analogy I use to explain that is, **"Giving a chef six eggs to make you lunch. You really fancy a soufflé and when lunch comes it's an omelette and you're disappointed."** However, the chef didn't get it wrong, you just didn't give him the relevant information. If you hand over the eggs with a clear request for a soufflé, that's what you'll get and everyone will be happy

An example of how this worked for me, in the past.

In 1999 I was teaching part time and working as an EFT practitioner part time. I knew that I needed to let go of the teaching, because it left me with not enough energy to grow the EFT practice, which was what really lit me up.

I did lots of tapping on **I can't, I'm not allowed, everyone will think I'm mad, it's not possible for me,** and so on!

In the end, I was really clear. This was absolutely what I wanted and I had to act as though it was happening. I told the universe, clearly, that I wanted to leave teaching at Easter, this was September and I needed a job that would replace the teaching income and leave me with energy to grow the EFT Practice. I had no idea how that was going to happen, I was just really clear that it was going to. And that clarity is the key. When you have that absolute complete clarity, everything works as you intend. If you're still hearing voices saying it can't happen, it just means there's more tapping to do, so do that.

Nothing happened for a few weeks, and I still knew, with certainty, that I was leaving teaching at Easter. I continually thanked the universe for sorting it for me.

And then it happened, someone asked me to take a celebration of life funeral. They had been asked to take it and couldn't and wanted me to stand in. I had no idea how to do that and they said they would talk me through it. My first thought was to back away and then I stopped. I'd already been brave about leaving teaching, maybe I could be brave about this too. So, I took the funeral. It was for a murder victim, we had an open coffin and I was on the TV news, all on my first funeral! Afterwards, her mother said to me, "That was perfect, I bet you've done thousands of these, haven't you?" I said, "No, it's my first." And she said, "Well you should be doing this, other people need it too." And I took the hint!

Lots more tapping and then I rang all the funeral directors in the county, told them I took celebration of life funerals and would they like to add me to their list, not even knowing if they had a list! Luckily the first person said yes, so I sat back and waited for something to happen ....and it didn't.

I waited and waited and Easter was getting closer and I didn't know what to do.

So, I took myself to the crematorium. I sat in the car, looking at the chapels and I imagined being part of it. I imagined knowing what goes on there, knowing everyone there, being part of the team. I saw it really clearly and most importantly I felt it. My heart opened and I loved everyone there, everyone that I would connect with. It felt so real, it was my reality in that moment. And then I went home, thanking the universe for me being part of that team, that reality. That was January and to leave at Easter, I had to resign at the end of February half term. I heard nothing until two weeks before half term, when I was booked for five funerals in half term week. Apparently, vicars go on holiday then, between Christmas and Easter! On the strength of that I resigned, and I'm endlessly grateful to my head teacher at that time, who supported me so much. By Easter I was taking three funerals a week, more than enough to cover my part time teaching salary. I continued with the funerals for three years, while I built my practice and then someone else took over for me and is still doing it now.

This is just one example of really being where you want to be and allowing yourself to connect clearly with how you feel in that situation. The times I've done that, I've always manifested what I intended and you can too. Remember, if something's not working, it just means something's in the way.

So, take some time to **play with this**, you could draw, you could write, you can really imagine being there and seeing what else you'd want. Sometimes, being there and allowing yourself to really feel how that would be gives you new information, so you can adjust your desires. And of course, if you get what you want and then find it's not what you really want, you just go through the process again. It's not a failure, it's a gathering of information

Vision boards can be a help in this process.

The last time I was doing a vision board, I had all the travel to lovely destinations on there. I had talking to large groups of people, friends and family. And it was only as someone looked over my shoulder and said it looks as though your house and garden are central to your life, that I realised that was what filled the whole centre of my board! I had no idea it was so important to me. I knew I loved gardens, I just hadn't realised about the house. At that point I was renting a house and a couple of years later, I was in my own house, with my own garden and I celebrate it every day.

When I was looking for a house, I wrote a "Thank you universe, for finding me a house with," and I listed all the things I wanted it to have. I also added, "and anything I've not thought of that I would like." I'd done that before, when I was looking for my rented house and it worked perfectly, so I was pretty sure it would work this time too. I'd almost given up on finding somewhere that had a garden I'd like, when a real estate agent dropped some details into my inbox and I thought, that's it. I went to visit on an open day and said to the estate agent, "Could I look at the garden first, as, if that doesn't work, I won't waste your time" and that was what got me the house. Although others offered more than me, the guy sold it to me as his dad had been a great gardener and he wanted it to go to someone who would look after it! Miracles really do happen!

When you've done this exercise, with or without a vision board and you have some clarity about what you'd like your life to be like, think about if you had all those things you want, in your life, **how would you feel? What would be different?**

Write down those feelings - are they peace, security, joy, contentment, something else? Keep them in mind because those are the feelings you'll want to start to attract into your life right now. You don't have to wait until your dreamed of life is in place, to feel those feelings, in fact feeling them right now will attract the things that you want quicker than anything else.

Here are some questions to help to focus you in.

How would you feel if all those things were in your life?

How would you be seeing yourself?

How would you be seeing the world?

What would you be doing differently?

And are there any voices telling you that you can't have that, for any reason? **If so, you could write them down to be tapped on.**

Let's tap together to start this process. This is really just setting things up, so that your subconscious has an idea of what you want to happen. You can also tap on any limiting beliefs that you notice.

> ***"Even though I didn't think my life could be like that, I'm OK."***
>
> ***"Even though I didn't think it was possible for my life to be like that, and maybe I believed that I didn't deserve to have my life like that, I'm open to the possibility that it would be ok, for me and everyone else."***
>
> ***"Even though I was limiting myself because I hadn't dared to look at what I really want, I've done that now and I'm***

really clear that those are the feelings I want."

"Whether I choose to attract all the things I've thought of into my life, or not, those feelings can be mine, right now and I'd like to instruct my Subconscious, to start attracting those feelings into my life right now."

"I'm choosing to no longer wait until all those wonderful things are in place. I choose to start making the changes right now, allowing myself to continue to take small steps, or giant leaps, or anything in between."

"I'd like the neural pathways that supported my old beliefs to begin to fade and new neural pathways that support my new feelings to grow and strengthen."

"I instruct my Subconscious to be alert to all possibilities of creating those new feelings in my life and to guide me easily, safely and comfortably into doing whatever has those feelings and I thank all Parts of me for their co-operation."

Now check in to see how it feels when you consider attracting that life. When you think about actually being there, and living it.

Notice and write down any negative beliefs or feelings that you notice, anything that doesn't feel comfortable and joyful.

When we have a clear desire for something and a Part of us believes it's not safe for us to have it, or we don't deserve it, or others won't like if we have it, we have Parts of us in conflict. One Part wants one thing and the other Part wants something else, usually the polar opposite.

This uses a huge amount of energy. One Part is pushing for one thing, and if it looks as though it might win, the other Part pulls in the opposite direction. All our energy is taken up by those Parts pulling backwards and forwards, just like the game of tug of war. If all Parts of us are in alignment, wanting the same things for us, all of our energy is free to take us forward to reach our goal. This is why it's so important for us to notice and clear anything that's in our way.

We can even do that by asking all Parts of us, directly, to get together and to find new ways of working that work for all Parts of us, so there is no conflict.

Let's tap

> *"Even though all Parts of me want the best for me and they're going about it in different ways and maybe no Part is getting what it really wants, I'd like to invite all Parts of me to get together and find new ways forward, that work for all of them and that are safer, healthier and much more fun that what they've been doing."*

You can also tap directly for those Parts that aren't sure how you're going to create the life you want.

> *"Even though I can't see how to create my life in that way.....yet....I choose to allow those Parts of me that know how to do it, to do it, out of my conscious mind, sharing the information with the rest of me and I thank them for their help and look forward with curiosity, to see what they create for me, in a safe, and healthy way."*

If you add in a safe and healthy way, and I often also add, that's much more fun, whatever's created will be better than what you had before.

One way to create changes more quickly, is to raise your vibration.

That basically means feeling better, about yourself, the world, what's going on for you.

One way to do that is to really focus on what's already worked well for you and to celebrate those things.

We're so used to focusing on what's not working and to beating ourselves up about what we haven't achieved, that we let our successes just pass us by, with no acknowledgement.

Here's an exercise to help to focus on the positive.

Look back over the last 10 years and take 15 minutes to write down what you're proud of.

Think about how you've changed.

Think about the things that have gone well.

Think of the people you've connected with positively.

Think about the times you've felt really connected to yourself.

Be as honest with yourself thinking of the

positives as you always are about the negatives.

When you've finished, allow yourself to be **pleasantly surprised,** you could even **allow yourself to be amazed,** by all the good things that have happened in your life.

And you can create more amazing things in your life right now.

We are all adding to the experience of the universe.

Whatever we want to experience, it's likely someone has felt it before and as we are connected to everything in the universe and to all times, past, present and future, we can borrow from what someone else has experienced, even if we haven't had experience of that ourselves.

When you think of what feelings would improve your life right now and would help you to create life as you want it, to be all that you can be, it can be useful to check if they are feelings that you've experienced before, in other situations. Often that will be the case.

Sometimes, the feelings you want to be feeling, you have no experience of, though you may have seen other people who seem to have them.

There are ways of accessing those feelings, even if they are new to you.

Imagine the Matrix, which contains everything. I imagine it rather like a web, connecting everyone and everything including source energy, so whatever has been experienced at any time, is available in the Matrix. You can imagine directly plugging into the energy of what it is that you want to feel/experience and imagine drawing it into yourself then check how it feels as you imagine yourself with access to those feelings that you want.

You can then imagine moving into the life you want to create, taking those feelings with you. How does that change things?

Another way to access the feelings that you want, is to think of who or what has those feelings. This could be a person or an animal. I had one trainee who connected to cat energy, as she was wanting to be in a place of being clear what she wanted and not being sucked into anyone else's needs. Someone else connected to an eagle, as they wanted to have that sense of freedom and also the ability to see the bigger picture, without being sucked into the small stuff. There's no one right way.

Allow yourself to be creative. If you can think of

something, you can do it.

Here is a link to a video on YouTube; https://youtu.be/Yt3-X-w7FrY **where I guide you through a visualisation of reconnecting to the essential, eternal part of you.**

Below is an approximate transcript of what I cover.

Close your eyes and take a few long, slow deep breaths.

Really feel who you are, feel your body. Call in any parts of you that have been missing, let them know that they're safe and welcomed and watch them coming back to join you, so the you that you are here and now, matches the eternal you that goes from life to life and isn't touched by any of the "stuff" from this life.

Really see who you are.

Envision living your life from that perspective.

Notice how differently you stand, breathe, move, talk, be.

Notice how differently and positively people respond to you.

Notice how easy it is to stay on track, to notice when something/someone is pulling you off balance and how easy it is to reconnect to you and get back on track without making it mean anything about you or anyone else.

Notice how much compassion you have for yourself and for the people around you

Really feel that you're doing the best you can, as you always do.

Notice how interesting and even exciting you find the challenges of living in a physical body.

Sense what an honour it feels to have that opportunity again and to contribute your experience to the universe so it's available for others to borrow.

Notice how much easier things seem and how struggle no longer seems the natural way forward.

Instruct your subconscious that this is the new way forward

Let it know that you want it to use these new feelings as a template for moving forward and that you want it to attract things into your life now, that will give you those feelings.

If at any time, these feelings are no longer working for your highest good, they can do something else, so long as it's safer, healthier and more fun than what it's been doing.

Celebrate the realization that you are you and in the right place, at the right time, with the right people, doing the right things.

You are perfect, whole and complete right now and you always will be.

Back to the Blueprint

Tap

1. Even though there is a blueprint within me, of the shining essence of me and I forgot that that is who I am, I deeply and completely love, accept and forgive myself.

2. Even though I forgot, I now gratefully accept help from my guides, helpers, angels, source, my higher self and all parts of me, to help and support, while cleaning, clearing and repairing all damage to my chakras, aura or any of my bodies, from this life and dimension, or any other, so that I return wholly to that shining, glowing essence of who I am.

3. Even though I forgot, I'm choosing now, to align to that blueprint of my shining essence and I ask that this is fuelled so that it continues, in ways that I don't need to know, continually clearing the connection to source and earth, so that I can continue to shine and glow and completely fill that me shaped space in the universe, that only I can use anyway. I ask with thanks and appreciation.

Thanks to Pika Rajner and Beth Sorger, for their parts in helping to create this.

And Finally

As I was writing this book, and oh what tapping opportunities it gave me! I had the realisation that, in the same way that I ask for help before a presentation on stage, I could ask for help while I'm writing the book, so I asked for a message for you, for our journey together and what came out was, of course, exactly what I needed to hear. I hope it is what you need to hear too.

From them and me, with love.

This is who you are! This is me, this is you, we are one.

A golden soul, eternal, powerful, wonderful, amazing, a great manifestor, the creator of worlds and realities. You are past, present and future and all of those are you. You are your sister, your brother, your neighbour, your mother, your boss, your father, your friend and your enemy.

You are everything. You are a part of everything and everything is a part of you. You and the rest are indivisible. What hurts you, hurts everything, what uplifts you uplifts

everything.

This is natural, normal, the way the world and the universe works.

Why are you here? To manifest the glory of God, however you see that energy, the endless possibilities, the multi-coloured versions of life. You're here to share your experience with all that is. You're here to grow and add to the colour of the world. You do that whatever you do, whether you choose struggle and fear, or ease and love, you are always doing your job. You are always right, you are always on target. And you can change your target anytime you choose. Don't look out to the world to see why that can't be true, why it doesn't work, look within and see how it can be true for you. In truth, there is only you and you are all and all is one.

You have power over yourself. You have power to choose, it you don't like what you're experiencing, no one will tell you that you have to keep on experiencing it. It's a world of free choice and it starts with you.

Your feelings are your guide. Listen to them, honour them, they are doing a valuable job. If you don't like what you're feeling, how can you change to a feeling you do like? When have you felt a good feeling before, reconnect with it, embrace it, enjoy it. Focus on every little bit of pleasure you can find. We watch you humans focus on what doesn't work, so hard. We watch you put all your energy into experiencing that and we wonder why. When there is so much good, so much love and happiness around you, you focus only on that and even then, it's ok. You have choice. If that's what you want to focus on you can, just know that you can focus on the other things too and with practice it will be just as easy.

You can only do it right. Whatever you do adds to the colours of the world. Everything that is or ever has been or will be is there, stored in the matrix for you to connect to, add to, amplify and if you can't find good feelings in your own life, borrow from others. Ask for what you need, it is there for you and will be given to you gladly. We are one, like those musketeers, one for all and all for one.

Your only job is to be you and that can be any version of you that you choose, just remember that underneath all the layers, the masks, the pretends, you are you, an indivisible part of god and the rest of the universe and all you need is yours and so you can ask for what you need at any time.

You may not remember, but I believe we chose this life and the people in it. You may wonder why, now, but at the time the choice was made, it was clear. You wanted experiences of the human world. You wanted to challenge yourself, you wanted to help those already here and those to come. You wanted to experience the joy of the beauty of this world. The life forms around you, the physical sensations. The feel of water on your skin, warm and welcoming, cold and challenging. You wanted the feeling of new grass beneath your feet and to feel the power of your body. You wanted to express things that you needed a body for. You wanted to use all your senses and the senses that aren't even known yet. You wanted to complete that cycle of physical and spiritual and you knew that, in spite of all you might choose to go through, ultimately it would be fun. Fun to touch and feel and sing and shout and run and play and work and love and hate and despair and feel joy and hope and wonder.

This is who you are! Enjoy your life, shine your light, it's what you came here for :)

Techniques Appendix

During this book, I will be talking about ways of working, some of which you may be familiar with, and some that you may not. I will talk about what works for me. You can adapt that to incorporate what works for you from your own practice and it would be good to experiment with different ways of working. That way you become much more flexible and open to your clients, if you have them, and to yourself, and you get to have some fun trying out combinations of techniques until you develop your own style.

My favourite technique, which I use with most clients, allows them to be very specific about their feelings, without knowing exactly what aspects are creating them, a form of bundling aspects together. It allows them to work content free if they choose and it's a great way to scale and keep track of changes.

Colour and shape technique

When you are in touch with an emotion that you would like to clear, ask

"Where are you feeling that in your body?"

It's a simple way of creating a label for the subconscious, so it knows what it's working on.

"If that feeling had a colour, what might it be?"

This phrasing allows you to consider possibilities without worrying about being right or wrong. Whatever is the first thing that pops into your mind.

Then check for **texture, sound, movement.**

Put all of that into a statement and you will be on the **bulls eye** and you don't even need to know what it's all about.

> ***"Even though I have this hard, red knot in my stomach, I deeply and completely accept myself."***

Keep following the feelings, wherever they move to, whatever they look like, until you are feeling comfortable.

EFT and Timelines

Using the colour/shape technique to go back to early events.

When you have a really clear feeling, or image

that is attached to what you want to work on, you can use this to take yourself back to an earlier time when you had that same feeling. This is where you need to working on the early logs in the log jam.

If you close your eyes and really be with that feeling, just imagine floating above your life and float back into the past to an earlier time when you had that same feeling. It might even be back in childhood.

You may come up with several events, choose the earliest and work on that and you can phrase the statement in such a way that you tell the subconscious that you are working on that or anything like that.

> ***"Even though I had this feeling or this hard, red knot in my stomach, when dad shouted at me when I was 3 and I probably had it many times before and since, I deeply and completely love and accept myself."***

This is telling the subconscious that all of these events are linked by this feeling and therefore they all need to be worked on. It's a great way of bundling baggage. You clear that early event and then check back to see how the clearing has impacted the current event.

Talking to the subconscious

The subconscious is always doing its best for you. Its job is to look for patterns in your life and repeat them for you, so that you don't have to do them consciously. That's very useful if you're talking about walking or chewing your food but much less useful if you are talking about having panic attacks.

The subconscious doesn't reason if what it does is useful. Once it does something it will continue to do it, unless you tell it to do something else. It's very obliging - ask it to do something else and it will, providing it doesn't think it will be dangerous.

It is quite easy to talk to the subconscious directly. In the past I would have had conversations with the subconscious while a client was in hypnosis. These days, I tap while we have the conversation and it works even better, because you can have a dialogue with the subconscious and the client and make adjustments and compromises, as necessary.

I spend most of my time with the client tapping on the karate point. I find that it's unobtrusive, the client gets into a rhythm, which is trance like, and it allows emotions to rise and process as we tap, bringing up new information and insights and generally keeps things flowing. I may have lots of conversations with the subconscious while we're on the point and then at the end, do a round on the rest of the shortcut points. You might like to try it and see how it works for you.

You can tap the karate point while you acknowledge your reality.

> ***"Even though it feels like my mum hates me, and that's the truth, I deeply and completely accept myself."***

Just saying and that's the truth, stops the part that didn't feel heard from fighting back.

You can then state how that feels, what effects it's had and what you'd like the subconscious to do instead. Give it new information that it's not had before, or not noticed.

> ***"Even though that's the truth for me and it really hurt and it still hurts now, that was then and this is now and maybe I don't need to stay stuck with those feelings. "***

> ***"Even though I've had those feelings for so long, I instruct my subconscious to release the need for them and to create new ways of feeling and being that are***

safer, healthier and much more fun than feeling hurt." (You could also add, Because that's what I deserve, if it seems appropriate.)

It's a great way to add reframes, just to have a conversation about what is, and then add other possible ways of seeing what is. Tapping really helps the reframes to land.

If you think about it as having a conversation with a willing but misguided employee, or a confused child, you'll get the idea!

It's also possible to use simple techniques and conversations with the subconscious to clear old ancestral and family patterns, even when you don't know what they are, by using what Milton Erickson called "artfully vague language."

This means giving instructions to the subconscious in such a way, that it can take the general information that you give it and find where that fits in a more specific way for you.

You will already be familiar with that concept from Borrowing Benefits, when the subconscious makes links between what the client is working on and what the audience is working on.

Sometimes, just having a conversation with

the subconscious, stating the facts, as the middle part of the EFT statement can be really powerful. Something about stating what is, or what might have been the truth and loving and accepting yourself anyway, seems to allow the subconscious to find what needs to be worked on and do it for you.

This does mean that it is not always possible to scale what you are working on at that time and it's important to know that the test is real life. How is your life different after the session?

Often you won't know what exactly has been worked on, but you will feel differently, the world will look different and you will find yourself reacting differently to situations that would have been a problem for you in the past.

The Box Technique

If you're running out of time to complete the work that is needed, either for yourself, or a client, it's possible to store the unfinished business safely.

> ***"Even though there's unfinished business and I don't have time to complete it now, I'm OK."***

> ***"Even though I don't have time right now, I instruct my subconscious to store the unfinished "stuff" safely, until the next time it's safe to work on it, or it can be worked on out of my conscious mind, with my thanks.***

Then imagine storing it in a container, and putting it somewhere safe. It can be in anything from a plain wooden box, to a bejewelled casket or anything that pops into your mind. This allows your subconscious to relax about what's not finished, knowing it can be safely stored, although often when you come back to it, you'll often find it's been sorted, without your conscious participation, which is a real bonus.

Quantum Physics, Epigenetics and the New Biology

Quantum physics, the new biology and epigenetics are all contributing to a new understanding of our world. There are many books out there that share this information and you'll find some suggestions of books you may find interesting in the bibliography in the book.

It is being said that this is a holographic universe, that we contain everything that has ever happened, or will happen within us.

It's said that everyone and everything is connected, some people refer to the energy that we are connected by as the Field, or the Matrix, or just the Universe.

Scientists have been investigating the theory that time may not be linear, it's possible that everything is happening at the same time. This means that any change now will change not just your future, but your past too and, maybe even other people's past lives.

Quantum Physics tells us that this is a world of vibration, that us and everything we see is just energy vibrating at different speeds. The faster the vibration, the more insubstantial the thing appears.

Like attracts like they say and Quantum Physics proves that's the case. Have you ever heard anyone say, "Do I have sucker stamped on my forehead?" or something similar? The answer is that if they are giving out the vibration of sucker, they will draw someone into their lives that will be a perfect match for them. Thus, the victim will attract the bully, the unconfident person will attract someone who will amplify the lack of confidence and at the other end of the scale, the person who is truly confident in who they are, is comfortable with their own power, will attract someone who will support them in that way.

The good news is that as you change your vibration it's possible to change the people that are drawn into your life.

There is more scientific proof than ever, that what the ancients believed, that all is one, is true. And if that's the case, we have access to all points of view, all resources, all experiences that anyone has ever had and we can use that to make changes for ourselves. And as we change ourselves, change happens around us. We have the capability to make the world anew, right here and right now. We are co-creators of the universe.

So join me in creating a vital, loving and joyous universe, for all to share!

Bibliography

David Hamilton	Destiny vs Free Will I <3 Myself How Your Mind Can Heal your Body
Bruce Lipton	Biology of Belief
Gregg Braden	The Divine matrix The Spontaneous Healing of Belief Fractal Time
Esther and Jerry Hicks	The Abraham Books
Arntz, Chase and Vincente	What the Bleep
Rhonda Byrne	The Secret
Dr Emoto	Messages from Water
Louise Hay	You Can Heal Your Life

Acknowledgements

I'd like to thank all who've been part of this wild ride, called life.

Peter Delves who started me on this healing journey, teaching me hypnotherapy, NLP and EFT. Meg and Elisabeth, my early tapping buddies.

Gary Craig for creating EFT and giving it so freely in the early days of EFT.

All my friends and colleagues that I've tapped with and learned from over the years, the other EFT Masters and especially Brad and Mel, who reminded me who I was and what was possible.

My wonderful clients, who have taught me so much. Sylvia my current tapping buddy extraordinare. It's a good job we've never added up the hours we've spent tapping :)

Rachel, Reema and Sylvia for proof reading and Clare, whose support and encouragement on writing this book is what's got it written and into your hands!

000

Printed in Great Britain
by Amazon

77166094R00088